DISCOVERY

HOW TO BECOME A CHAMPION
IN BUSINESS AND LIFE

MATT PHILLIPS
and
RUBEN GONZALEZ

DEDICATION

First and foremost, I thank God for His guidance, leadership, forgiveness, and above all else, His GRACE! I am unbelievably blessed with an amazing family, friends, and life experiences, and it is all attributable to God.

This book is dedicated to my loving wife and three amazing children!

My Message to My Family

As I write this book, my children are 7, 5, and 1 years old. I have coached my two older children in soccer and baseball so far, and I will continue to coach all of my children as they get older. Sports were a huge part of my life and I believe they will also play an important part in your life.

I write this book so that my children and wife would have a little piece of me to always take with them. I wanted to tell them about my life and some stories from the so-far 35 years of my life. I want them to know and understand what lessons I have learned from playing sports and how I now apply them to life.

I want them to know that God is always with them – the one constant in life. All you have to do is turn around and God will be walking right behind you. He will have a smile on his face because you are His most perfect creation! Whether you experience success or failure along the way, take time to pray to God and get to know Him. He will ALWAYS be with you! His love never fails!

Most of all, I want my kids to always know that I love them and I will always love them...NO MATTER WHAT! This life will present us with seemingly insurmountable challenges, but if we stick together as a family, with God at the core, we will triumph over any adversity in our lives.

Love,
Dad

CONTENTS

INTRODUCTION

Are you a champion in your life? In your business? With your team? With your kids? With your significant other? With your friends and other family? Are you a champion in your spiritual life?

It is difficult to answer these answers, unless you take the time to define "champion." How does society define it? More importantly, what does it mean to you?

A champion is a person who has defeated others in competition. We use such words as champ, victor, titleholder, and winner.

A champion is also defined as a person who defends a person or a cause, or a warrior who did battle for another to defend their rights or honor. We use such words as defender, guardian, backer, advocate, protector, upholder, promoter, and supporter.

A disconnect exists in society today about who a true champion is, whether in sports, business, or life. We place people on a pedestal who have that championship trophy or make gobs of money. Our societal definition of success is money and power, and we put championship crowns on those people, whether they deserve it or not.

The fact is that "champion" is neither about money, nor about power. It is about a belief that we can be a champion in everything we do, from the simplest things at home to the most complex business transaction. It is about approaching each part of our life with an unwavering focus and dedication to do the best we can with what God has blessed us with. It is about taking advantage of our talents, and working as hard as we can to maximize whatever we are trying to do. It is about being able to look in the mirror at the end of the day and say, "I gave it all I had today."

This book, "Discovery – How to Become a Champion in Business and Life," provides the key tips on how to be that champion in business and life. It focuses on lessons that Ruben and I learned through sports and on how to be successful in life and business by putting these lessons into practice.

I am a former Division-1 college baseball player in the United States and a Bundesliga ("first league") professional baseball player in Europe. Ruben is a four-time Olympian in luge and former college soccer player. We have endured the ups and downs that sports bring, and we now use the lessons learned from the sporting field to be champions in our own lives and businesses.

Each chapter begins with my story and my lessons, followed by Ruben's experiences: "A Message from Ruben Gonzalez."

This book represents a little piece of Ruben and me, and we hope that what you learn from our experiences may inspire and give you hope and direction in your life, whether in sports, life, or business.

Awards don't matter…your determination, belief, drive, and God-given abilities do! Look yourself in that mirror and say "I gave it everything I had today."

Go be a champion!

1
BECOME UNSTOPPABLE

"Energy and persistence conquer all things."
– Benjamin Franklin

As I sat with my parents during the beginning of my sophomore year of high school, I looked at them and said, "I don't want to play football anymore." I remember my parents asking me why I did not want to play, and I can't honestly remember how I answered that question. What I do remember, though, was that I felt intimidated by the other football players and didn't feel like I could play with them. I think my parents knew deep down that sometimes you have to let your kids make choices, whether you agree or not. Well, my parents let me decide that day and I never played football again.

Looking back, I am filled with regret. I can't believe that I let others intimidate me and take away what could have been a great time in my life. I let myself down because I did not fight for what I wanted. I had the physical ability to play football, but I let the mental side of that obstacle grow so big that it seemed like I would never be able to conquer it. So, I quit. I backed down instead of fighting back.

Throughout life, we will face seemingly insurmountable challenges, roadblocks, and difficulties as we drive toward our dreams and ambitions. The beauty is that we have a choice on how we respond. We can let that obstacle push us into giving up and relinquishing or we can fight, persevere, and pursue our goals with unrelenting passion.

By deciding to persevere and drive towards your goals no matter what mountain you have to climb, you will truly be unstoppable!

I BELIEVE IN ME!

"No one can make you feel inferior without your consent." –
Eleanor Roosevelt

My biggest struggles while playing sports were injuries and from what you read above, confidence. I remember twisting my ankle horribly during my junior year of college, which side-lined me for two weeks. I wanted so badly to get back on that field quickly, but instead I was stuck rehabbing. I worried that the injury would hurt my playing time. I wondered if I would be able to run at full strength ever again.

Because of my passion for playing baseball and my drive to get back on that baseball field, I focused

2

on my rehab and did everything I could to heal my ankle. Two weeks later, I picked up right where I left off on that baseball field. It was my focus and belief in myself that helped me to overcome this roadblock. I had confidence that I would heal. That injury would not hold me back.

Now in business, as I continue to expand my speaking business and non-profit organization, I believe in myself and what I am trying to do. I decide what is important enough for me to fight for in my life and I go after it. I try to ignore the distractions and focus on what is truly important. I focus on my faith, family, career, and health. When I come up against any obstacle in those areas, I keep pushing and pushing with my eye securely focused on my goal.

(Me doing what I love most…helping people by speaking)

Whether or not you are an athlete, you need to decide what is important in your life. Then you push for what you want and need, and keep your eyes fixed on your goals.

If athletics is important and you are trying to make a team or get to the Olympics, focus your mind, body, and spirit on that end goal and get it done.

Keep stepping in that batter's box. Keep swinging that bat. You will hit that ball eventually. Persist. Push.

For those things that are important to you, continue to believe in yourself and show unrelenting determination as you push towards achieving your goals. Become unstoppable!

PEOPLE WHO BELIEVE IN YOU!

"We find comfort among those who agree with us – growth among those who don't." – Frank A. Clark

Believing in yourself is the first thing you need to do. But, in order to truly be successful in your life or in achieving your goal, you also need people who believe in you!

You need people on your side who will motivate you, drive you, challenge you, and be there when you need them. The amazing thing about people who care about you is that they will be there as you climb up that mountain and face that obstacle, and sometimes they will be there to tell you that you are on the wrong mountain all together. They become accountable to you and you to them.

These people bring a different perspective on what you are going through. It always amazes me how different people's perspectives are when facing an obstacle. What may seem like a small obstacle to one person may seem like a HUGE one for another person. When my parents were sitting there listening to me tell them I did not want to play football anymore, I am sure they were thinking that it was not that big a deal. "Go out and play football" is what I am sure they were saying in their heads. But to me, it was a huge deal. It was a mental block that I could not overcome…or at least I thought that at the time.

I wish I had been able to really put my mental struggle in perspective at that time. I wish I had been able to properly size my struggle, because at the end of the day, the mountain I had made in my mind was nothing close to that.

Now that I am a father, I see my kids struggle with similar things. Just the other day, my daughter was telling me how she did not want to swim anymore because at the next level, you have to learn how to do kick turns at the wall. That scares her because of going under water and not being able to breathe. She is a great swimmer for seven years old. I know that she will be able to do those kick turns in the pool and will be fine. My perspective is so much different than hers though. She sees it from her vantage point, and I see it from mine. I have life's lessons to draw upon and I know she can do it, but she just doesn't know it yet.

Perspectives can be deceiving. You must seek out other perspectives on your obstacle!

I started to finally do this in college with sports and I do it now in business and while raising children. I have built up a network of individuals whom I trust with all my heart, including my wife, parents, sister, uncles, and best friend. When I am faced with a tough time in my life, I go to these individuals to hear their perspective…to listen!

It is crucial to seek out trusted perspectives on whatever you are facing. Lean on those you love and trust. If you don't have people like that in your life, start seeking those people out. Start building that core of individuals who will give you perspectives you can trust.

And as for my daughter doing kick turns, because I believe in her and fight for her, I will continue to motivate her, challenge her, and most importantly, love her! She will conquer those kick turns…she will be unstoppable!

ACTION ITEMS

Let's put these lessons into action! Please take some time to reflect on the following:

- Do you believe in yourself? Why or why not?

- Write down two goals you have and answer the following questions:

  - Do I have the personal belief to achieve my goal? How can I believe in myself even more?

  - Do I have the right people around me who believe in me? Who are they? If not, who can I seek out?

A WORD FROM RUBEN GONZALEZ

"How to Become Unstoppable"

Most luge athletes start when they are eight to ten years old. Ten-year-olds are bulletproof. They are not afraid of anything. And by the time they are old enough to know better, they have developed such great skills that they hardly ever experience any fear.

But I got started in the sport of luge when I was twenty-one. I luged for 27 years and have thousands of runs under my belt, but until the last couple of years I was scared after every single run.

After all, you're hurtling down an icy chute at 80-90 MPH pulling up to 6 Gs on the tight corners. I never liked it. It was too scary. But it did not matter if I liked it. The luge was my ticket to the Olympics.

The fear was so strong that I wanted to quit after every run. Fortunately, there's a saving grace at the bottom of the track. A walkie-talkie I used to talk to my coach.

My coach is a four-time Olympian and a three-time World Champion. He's the Michael Jordan of luge.

(Coach Guenther and I in Germany)

When I pick up the walkie-talkie, in 30 seconds Coach does two things: he tells me what I did wrong and how I can be faster the next time, and in my case, more importantly, he encourages me to keep fighting for my Olympic dream. He helps me take my focus away from my fear and focus on the dream - The Olympics.

You will have bad days in your life. You'll have bad weeks, bad months, and once in a while, even a bad year. When you're struggling, when you're going through life's storms, don't try to figure things out by yourself. If you do, you'll always take the easy way out, quit, and regret it later.

Rather, do what I did. Pick up the walkie-talkie. Pick up the phone. Call someone who loves you. Call someone who believes in you. Call someone who will get you back on your sled. Call someone who will get you back on track. Call someone who will not let you quit.

If you quit on your dream, you'll regret it all your life.

Action Item Notes

Action Item Notes

2
FIND BALANCE
THROUGH IMBALANCE

"Next to love, balance is the most important thing."
— John Wooden

Playing baseball in college presented one of the toughest personal challenges in my life. Along with about 3-4 hours of baseball practice and conditioning per day, I needed to commit time to class and homework, class projects, friends, church, calls with family back in Colorado, etc. All of a sudden the extra time that seemed to exist in high school was swallowed up by all of these responsibilities and activities. I remember thinking to myself, "How am I supposed to do all this stuff?"

I became overwhelmed with all the things I had to do, whether for sports, school, or other areas. I realized that I could not do everything at once and that I needed to find a new balance in my life.

Maintaining balance is challenging. We read books about balance, and it is usually defined as being well-rounded and having spiritual, physical, and mental strength. You hear about giving enough time to everything that is important to you, like working, staying in shape, spending quality time with your family, eating right, going to church, having a nice car and house…here we go again with the long list.

The fact is that if you want to be successful in business, sports, or life, you must first understand that you cannot do everything at once and that *balance is achieved through imbalance*! We cannot fit everything in that we want to do. We cannot achieve everything at once. We find balance through imbalance, and imbalance is achieved through prioritization, organization, and efficiency in each particular season of life.

EVERYTHING HAS A SEASON

"The key to keeping your balance is knowing when you've lost it." – Anonymous

With all that we have to do in life, does it make sense that you can do everything at once? Can you be as great as you want at each thing when you try to pack it all in? Can you excel at everything you have to do and want to do?

If we try to fit everything in at once and think we can do a great job, we are just fooling ourselves. We end up spinning our wheels as we think of everything we need to do because we want to be well-rounded. We want others to see us as balanced people.

Instead of balancing everything, we must understand that there is a season for everything in our lives, just like the seasons we experience on earth (summer, fall, winter, spring). We have to live in seasons in order to be successful. We need to give everything we can to each season of our life. Inevitably, ebbs and flows will follow as we determine what takes precedence in our lives.

As it says in Ecclesiastes in the Bible:

There is a time for everything,
and a season for every activity under the heavens:
a time to be born and a time to die,
a time to plant and a time to uproot,
a time to kill and a time to heal,
a time to tear down and a time to build,
a time to weep and a time to laugh,
a time to mourn and a time to dance,
a time to scatter stones and a time to gather them,
a time to embrace and a time to refrain
from embracing,
a time to search and a time to give up,
a time to keep and a time to throw away,
a time to tear and a time to mend,
a time to be silent and a time to speak,
a time to love and a time to hate,
a time for war and a time for peace.

Whatever season of life you are in, give it your all! Take out that list of to-do's, scrap it, and start over by writing down what is important to you. List your top priorities and then throw your time and energy at them.

By prioritizing, organizing, and utilizing your time efficiently, you will set yourself up for success!

PRIORITIZATION

"Most people struggle with life balance simply because they haven't paid the price to decide what is really important to them." – Stephen Covey

Before you do anything else, you must figure out what is important in your life. What season of life are you in right now? What is most important to you? What do you need to focus on to be successful in life?

For me, school, baseball, family, and friends were on the top of my priority list during college. Everything else came after. If I had an opportunity to go to a party, for example, but I knew that my homework needed to be done, then I would prioritize homework over the party. In order to be successful, I needed to hold fast to my priorities.

The same can be said in this season of my life. I am married with three children and work a full-time job. I have four top priorities in my life right now: Faith, family, career, health. I want to spend time with my wife and children. As the financial provider for my family, I need to do well at my job. As the spiritual leader of my family, I want to have a strong faith and be a good example for others. If I have a chance to go to a baseball game for example, but I have not spent time with my wife and children, then perhaps I sacrifice the game for more important things.

Am I saying you should never have a good time? Absolutely not. I am saying that you need to make sure to address your top priorities first before going onto those secondary options. If my homework was done in college, then I might go to a party. I knew though that I wanted good grades in school so I could land a good job eventually. That commitment to my education became much more important than the party.

Your top priorities should be ones that set you up for ultimate success in your life, and should be driven by the season of life you are in.

ORGANIZATION

Once you have your priorities in order, you need to organize your time and determine what can be done and when.

During college, I carried an organizer (calendar) where I wrote down what I needed to accomplish and when, such as my class schedule each day, when baseball practice started and ended, and when and how long I had to study that night. I made a list of my homework and crossed them off as I completed each task. I learned quickly that I had to do this to ensure that I stayed focused on what needed to be accomplished each day. Writing it down also helped me keep my priorities in order and focused on my goals.

I apply a similar approach in my life today, whether in my personal or professional life. My wife and I discuss what we need to do each week. We talk about spending time with children, work, kid's sports schedules, etc., and then typically write it down so we are organized. We talk about our future and what our goals are as a couple, family, financially, and spiritually, and make sure that we take the necessary steps.

In business, I take the priorities I have identified and focus on organizing the steps I need to take to accomplish my goals. I make sure I understand all the steps to be successful, and then determine a timeline and necessary resources. This allows me to track my end goal, have forward motion towards it, and be aware of the bridges I need to cross to reach achievement.

If you don't keep track of what you need to accomplish and the steps to get there, you will be trying to find a destination with no map. Organize your life and prepare that map for your success!!

EFFICIENCY

"A particular shot or way of moving the ball can be a player's personal signature, but efficiency of performance is what wins the game for the team. " – Pat Riley

While it is great that you know your priorities and are organized, you need to go one step further and actually use your time wisely! You need to be efficient with your time and execute!

For example, at Creighton, our baseball coach would post the practice schedule in the dugout before each practice . Coach Servais would actually show 3 minutes on one drill, 4 on another. It was amazing. He squeezed every minute out of every practice by ensuring our time was utilized efficiently.

Using your time efficiently can be applied to any task or area in your life. It could be while practicing your sport, studying, working, praying, etc. You need to squeeze out every minute in everything you are doing to take advantage of the time you have. You need to look for new ways to be efficient so you can be successful in achieving your goal.

ACTION ITEMS

Let's put these lessons into action! For this season of your life, write down the top five important things to you (work, home, spiritual items), and reflect on the following:

- Are you spending the appropriate time on these five items, or are you distracted by other items?

- Are you organizing your time to ensure that you are spending the appropriate time on these five items? How can you be better organized?

- Are you being efficient with your time when approaching these five items? How can you be more efficient?

A WORD FROM RUBEN GONZALEZ

"What's Important to You Right Now?"

A reporter asked Thomas Edison how he could be so incredibly productive. After all, Edison had over 1000 patents. Edison answered, "I focus 100% on one thing until I am finished with it. Then I move on to the next thing." Multi-tasking does not work. It just wastes time.

Most people don't understand what living a balanced life means. They try to equally balance everything in their lives and as a result they never accomplish anything and end up regretting it later. That kind of balance is what Jesus called living a lukewarm life. Believe me, you don't want your life to be lukewarm. You want it to be sizzling hot.

If you want your life to be exciting, fun and sizzling, you need to be purposely unbalanced. Purposeful unbalance is the only way to reach a higher level whatever you do. Purposeful unbalance means you dedicate more time and effort to whatever is most important to you right now.

To outsiders you'll look unbalanced. They'll say you are driven. They may even call you a fanatic. But they are wrong. You are simply focusing on what's important to you at this point in your life.

When I was in high school and college my focus was school and soccer. Mainly soccer. I played soccer every minute I could. People must have thought I was a soccer fanatic. I played on Houston Baptist University's NCAA Division I team and that was the big focus in my life.

Then, after my junior year, I decided to take up the sport of luge and qualify for the 1988 Calgary Winter Olympics. A goal of that caliber would take a huge commitment. All of a sudden soccer was not that important. I actually quit the soccer team to focus 100% on the luge. How many athletes with an athletic scholarship would be willing to quit their sport in order to try to achieve a new dream? But I had to quit soccer in order to free up time for the luge.

What's important to you right now? Are you dedicating enough time to it? If not, you're fooling yourself. Concentration of effort is a big part of success.

After college between 1988 and 2002, work and the luge were my priorities. After the 2002 Salt Lake City Olympics, I was invited to speak at a school. The Principal said I needed to speak professionally because I had a gift. I had always wanted to own my business. At the time I sold copiers in Downtown Houston, but I quit my job and quit the luge in order to build a speaking business. People told me I was crazy. But I had a new dream...To own my own business.

It was a new season. For six years (2002 - 2008) I worked tirelessly to build a successful business - 12 to 18 hour days. People told me I was crazy to work so hard. But I simply focused on my new dream. To create a business that would give me the option to live wherever I wanted to live, work out of my home, and spend time with my family.

After six years, my business was really strong and I shifted gears again. I decided to get back into the luge and to try to qualify for a 4th Olympics - Vancouver 2010. I wanted to show people that if you want something badly enough, age does not matter. For two years the luge again became a big focus. I competed in the Vancouver Olympics at the age of 47. Everyone thought I was a coach. The kid that won the Gold Medal in the men's luge was not even born when I was competing in the 1988 Calgary Olympics.

After competing in Vancouver, a new season in my life began. Today my new season is spending maximum time with my family. My office is out of my home, and we home school our children. My main focus today is to create memories with my kids as I teach them the values that will help them live fruitful lives.

See how with some planning, focus and hard work you can create your ideal life? You just have to decide you will do it.

So as you can see, life balance is not about balancing your life. It's about determining what's important in each season of your life and focusing on that thing. It's just like Curly said in the movie City Slickers, "What's the one thing that's most important to you?"

So what's important to you right now? Focus on it for this season and give it your all. You'll be glad you did.

(84 MPH at the Salt Lake City Olympics)

Action Item Notes

Action Item Notes

3
COMPETE, COMPETE, COMPETE

"If you're a competitive person, that stays with you. You don't stop. You always look over your shoulder."
– Magic Johnson

I am the kind of guy who is competitive in everything I do. Whether it is in sports, at work, or playing board games at home, I like to win. It is just something inside of me that makes me want to score more points, hit the ball farther, or become better at my job than other people.

Now to say that I always did score more points, hit the ball further, or am better at my job than others, well, that would be a blatant lie. Some days this did and does happen, of course, but one thing I know is that I certainly try at all times to be the best I can be and use my competitive attitude to my advantage. I still employ this "working hard" attitude today.

Playing sports has taught me a lot about what a competitive attitude should look like and how to use it in a positive, future-focused way. In sports, life, and business, we need to bring a work ethic and intensity that is unmatched and unrivaled, but we also must ensure that our desire to win is focused on something that we believe in!

INTENSITY AND WORK ETHIC

"A lot of times I find that people who are blessed with the most talent don't ever develop that attitude, and the ones who aren't blessed in that way are the most competitive and have the biggest heart." – Tom Brady

As a walk-on to the Creighton baseball team, I found myself constantly having to prove myself on the field. I had to find a way to get noticed by the coaches so I could improve my skills and get some playing time. I think college was when my competitive attitude really blossomed.

I discovered that I had to constantly bring intensity and a strong work ethic to the field every single day. I had to consistently show up and give it everything I had so that I would be ready when my opportunity arose. I needed to prove to the coaches that I deserved to make the team. Intensity and work ethic! I knew I had to outwork everyone on that field if I was to ever see the field during a game.

I encountered guys all the time who had more talent than me but who didn't have my drive or attitude during practice or in games. The ones I would see go on to the next level and beyond had a mix of incredible talent, intensity, and work ethic. You can see examples of these types of guys in professional sports. Look at Tim Tebow, Peyton Manning, Phil Mickelson. We remember the names of these people because they are consistent in how they approach games or practice, and they constantly push to improve. Talent will only get you so far, while intensity and work ethic make up for the rest.

Whether at work or at home, you need to look inside yourself and ask if you are doing everything you can to maximize the talent God gave you. Are you working as hard as you can? Are you giving it your all? Are you approaching each life situation with a consistent intensity and focus? If you answered "no" to even one of these questions, you are cheating yourself and your talent. You need to look in the mirror and decide if you are all in or not.

I have chosen the approach of working as hard as I can in every facet of life. My high intensity and incredible work ethic drives the expansion of my speaking business. It pushes me when raising my children and teaching them to be the best individuals that they can be. I put them into practice in my faith and in my marriage.

Do what you can with what you've got! Bring that intensity! Work your tail off! Be consistent!

BELIEF IN WHAT WE ARE DOING

While it is nice to work hard in life, I have found that my competitive attitude is at its peak of intensity when I fully believe in what I am doing. Do you find that same thing?

I have been in situations, whether with a particular team or job, where I did not feel like giving 110% and I wasn't willing to bring my full intensity. As I think about it, it all came down to a lack of passion…a lack of belief in what I was doing.

Throw me into a situation where I believe in the team, company, activity, etc., and watch out! I will leave everything on the field or in the meeting room. I will give everything I have. I will bring my passion, intensity, and work ethic which are truly unmatched.

I have to make sure as a business owner, leader, team member, father, husband, etc., that I am passionate about what I am doing and believe in where we are going. That is when I am all-in! And with my business, my teams, my family, and my marriage, I am 110% in!

I moved to Austria to play baseball in the Bundesliga (first league) on an all-Austrian team during college. During the first few practices, it was clear to me that this team did not have the same level of experience as I did. The first few games were painful, both for me and the team. I was playing horribly and so was the team. I began to question if I truly believed in this team.

I spent a tremendous amount of time reflecting on this issue, and what I eventually came to realize was that I needed to change my approach on the field. I needed to bring the team together and to help us all believe in our ability on the field. I shifted my focus to the team and helping them improve their baseball skills. I started to believe in this team and used my intensity and work ethic to build up everyone else on the team so we ALL could become better. We worked on fielding drills, hitting drills, throwing drills, etc., all in an effort to take our team to the next level. We started improving. We started believing that we could win games!

I am so proud that we ended up with the best record in the league for the second half of the season!

(Article in local Austrian newspaper about one of my games)

As I look back at this situation, my lack of belief in the team at first clouded my judgment and attitude. I started to doubt my team and lose focus on what I was doing. Because of some good advice from my father (don't you hate it when your parents are right???), my vision and thoughts were cleared and I was able to finally see the ways I needed to contribute to make us successful and win some games.

Find something that you believe in, whether at work or at home, and then unleash your intensity and work ethic! Don't let your lack of belief cloud your judgment or attitude. Refocus yourself on something that you believe in and then go after it! The wins will take care of themselves.

ACTION ITEMS

Let's put these lessons into action! Reflect on the following items:

- In what areas of my life do I have the most intensity and work ethic? Why?

- In what areas of my life do I struggle to have intensity and work ethic? Why?

- What areas are important to me where I want to bring my full intensity and work ethic?

A WORD FROM RUBEN GONZALEZ

"A Dream that Takes Your Breath Away"

I was born in Argentina, which is a soccer-crazed nation. Every boy in Argentina thinks he's going to play World Cup soccer, and I was no different. Ever since I can remember, I played soccer. Unfortunately, I was never a great athlete. I can't run fast. I can't jump high, and I'm not particularly strong. So even though I had developed good soccer skills, I was still usually on the bench.

I was a walk-on for the Houston Baptist University soccer team, but most of the time I sat on the bench. I did everything I could to make myself valuable to the team so the coach would not cut me. Coach kept me on the team because he wanted the other players to see my competitive drive and ambition. I was the "Rudy" of the team.

(Warming up my soccer bench in college)

33

Being in the speaking business, I run into the real Rudy once or twice a year. We were having breakfast together a few years ago talking about our dreams. I told Rudy that I didn't like the sport of luge because it was too scary. I told Rudy the only reason I did the luge was because it was my ticket to the Olympics.

Rudy chuckled and said, "I didn't even like playing football. My dream was to be a part of the Notre Dame tradition and what better way to do that than to be a part of their football team."

Rudy's competitive drive helped him be a part of the Notre Dame tradition in the best way.

That's why you have to pursue what excites you, a dream that takes your breath away. When you do, your competitive spirit will come out and you will be on your way to creating a magnificent life.

Action Item Notes

Action Item Notes

4

GET READY FOR CHANGE…
IT'S COMING

Change…it truly is the only constant in life, isn't it? We experience it every day. Change appears in all different shapes and sizes and happens at every age. I handled change well in some cases and poorly in others. One of the biggest changes in my life left a lasting impact.

Tryouts

I was not highly recruited out of high school to play college baseball, so I decided to attend Creighton University in Omaha, Nebraska and try out (walk-on) for the baseball team. For two days of tryouts, bats were cracking, and balls were flying all over that field. It was an absolute thrill.

After the second day of tryouts, all of the walk-ons were called into the coach's office to find out if we made the team. I vividly remember walking into that office and sitting down with the head and assistant baseball coaches. To be honest, I don't remember too much of the conversation as they told me,

"Matt, we do not have a spot on the team for you this year." My mind went blank.

No baseball? You have got to be kidding me! I got cut? You have to be joking! I had played baseball nearly my entire life. "Baseball player" was my identity. When I told people what I did, baseball was the first thing I talked about. I expected to tell people that I was a college baseball player at Creighton University. In a flash, in a blink of an eye, "baseball player" vanished.

I quickly fell into a depression, and with all my free time (no baseball practice), I decided to fill it with alcohol…and partying. I started going to parties multiple nights a week and drinking quite a bit at those parties, because, for no other reason, it just seemed to fill the time.

The choices I made began to slap me in the face pretty quickly. Having played sports, I am a very competitive person, both with myself and with others. I liked getting good grades in school and doing well on the baseball field. I remember walking into a political science class a few months after getting cut from the baseball team and the professor handed back a paper with a terrible grade. I was angry! Not with him, but with me. How had I let my grades slip?

It was at that moment that I decided to take a deeper look inside myself. I was determined to figure out who I really was as a person and to start prioritizing the important things in my life. That grade was the trigger I needed to right the ship.

I stopped drinking alcohol from that moment on. I focused on my school work. I attended church to develop a relationship with God, asking Him to help guide my life. It jolted me to the core and finally forced me to face this change head-on. I started to deal with my emotions and what had happened when I got cut. I started to find ways to fill the void that baseball had left me.

DEALING WITH YOUR EMOTIONS

The first thing we have to do when going through a transition is to understand and actively deal with our emotions.

When I got cut from my baseball team, I decided to best deal with my emotions by talking with my Dad, Mom, and sister right away. I prayed for help through this tough time.

Later that night, I wrote down my thoughts and feelings about what had happened. Here is a copy of my letter:

Dear Family and Friends,

To my loving family that has provided guidance and strength in my life.

I am writing you today to tell you about my experience trying out for a Division One baseball team. The reason that I chose to thank all of you is that each person has inspired, taught and guided me in the game I love so much.

My baseball career ended today. I cannot describe the emotions that run through my mind right now. There is anger, sadness, and happiness. When I had my first tryout, I had an unsettled feeling in my stomach. I came to find out later what that feeling was.

It was that I had not shown what I could fully do with my potential. I hit the baseball very well, and my fielding was great. I first thought my uneasiness was my illness that I had the day of tryout, but it wasn't. It was like I was afraid to let go and show the coaches all that I am. I'll tell you what, I felt confident that day after I left the field. Not that I would make the team, but at the fact that I had worked hard. And you know what, I got called back the next day to be on the field for the coaches.

When I walked onto that field the second day, a feeling like no other sunk in. The complete baseball atmosphere was right there in front of me. Balls were flying, people were yelling, and players were having fun. This is a feeling that I cannot describe. I had a smile on my face the whole practice. I wondered what the other guys were thinking. This place was where I had dreamed of being, and now I was there. I was in the most special place in the world. I was trying out for a Division One ball club. How much better could it get? I passed the test I set for myself. I was hesitant about trying out all summer, but I did it and it felt great! I wouldn't trade that second practice for anything in the world.

I thank my batting coach and friend. You've taught me well, bud. You gave me inspiration and perspective that my family couldn't provide. Thank you for everything you have done to make my dreams come true.

Dad, you taught me this game. From day one, you were my coach, my idol. You brought baseball to my life. I love you, Dad! Thank you for allowing me to grow under your guidance.

Mom, what can I say about you? You were my guide through the tough times. While I was trying to tough out an injury or other situation, you were the person to come to and cry when I needed it. You and Dad are the world to me. I love you guys so much! You have given me the world. Thanks for teaching me to fly!

My big sister, always leading the way only to be followed by her little bro. You have set such a good example for me. One of the reasons I chose to come to school here was because you were here, and I knew it would be twice as good if you were here. You are my true best friend in life. Thank you.

To my extended family, you have shown me the true meaning of family. All of you have shown me new light and paths toward success. I love you all very much.

One thing that I have learned from this is that all of us must reach for our dreams. You know what my dream is? My dream is to play Division One baseball. You know what, I got that dream. I was out on a perfect field, on a perfect afternoon, and I was playing baseball. Though I am sad my career as a baseball player is over, I am happy. When a person reaches their dream, it is so sweet. Thank you everyone, and I love you. Baseball ended for me today. What a great feeling!

Love,

Your son, brother, grandson, nephew, and friend

Talking to trusted friends and family, writing down my thoughts and feelings, and praying was how I decided to positively work through the emotions I was experiencing. I am the kind of person who needs to release my emotions. If I hold them in, at some point, I explode. I need an "outlet."

If you are like me, then you need to talk to someone about the issue you are facing. Turn to the most trusted people in your life for those discussions and just share how you are feeling.

If you are a writer, get out a piece of paper or your laptop and write down your feelings. You may find crying, laughing, praying, running, or many other positive ways to deal with your emotions. Get everything out on the table. Pour out your emotions. Find your "outlet."

Negative Temptations

You have a choice about how you will react when faced with a life transition. Do you want to give into alcohol, drugs, and other negative temptations that numb your emotions and paralyze you? You can go to ESPN and search for stories on depression, suicide, drugs, and alcohol, and you will have days filled with examples and stories on how individuals have given into negative temptation and how it has destroyed their lives.

Instead of giving into these temptations, you need to ask yourself, "Now that sports (or my job, or a loved one, etc.) are gone, am I going to give in to the world's negative temptations? Or am I going to make positive choices and changes in my life? Am I going to positively or negatively deal with my emotions?"

When I got cut from the baseball team, I chose a negative path by allowing alcohol into my life. Alcohol paralyzed me. It did not allow me to deal with my emotions or really move on with my life. I am so thankful that I was able to recognize that and right my ship.

Please, please, take time today to build your plan for how you most effectively and positively will handle your emotions.

FILL THE VOID

After getting cut from the baseball team, I clearly struggled with how to fill the void that existed. I had always identified myself with sports and now that identity was gone, and I did not understand what my identity was going to be in the future. It was through self-discovery and a lot of work that I finally started to discover other interests in life and other ways to give me the same feelings and enjoyment that I experienced with baseball. You may be struggling right now with emptiness or a void in your life that needs to be filled, or life may seem good. In any case, my advice would be to start making a plan right now! Life may seem all good right now, however, you never know when things can and will change. Formulate your plan before it happens!

Inevitably, priorities shift when you experience a change or transition in your life. You will have to re-look at what is important in life and make an adjustment for what takes top precedence at that point. For example, if you lose a loved one and you were used to spending a lot of time with them, you need to figure out how to positively fill that void.

Get out a piece of paper or laptop or iPad and start writing down your interests. Never stop writing and thinking…your interests always change. And remember to refer to this list whenever you hit a stopping point in life or in sports.

I now challenge myself in other ways, but sports are always in there somewhere. I do P90X, ski, and coach my children in sports. I work in a career that challenges me and brings out my competitive spirit. Fortunately, this world has so much to offer and so many opportunities that continue to shape my life in positive ways.

The thing is…I don't think of that void much anymore…I just get excited thinking about what I am going to do next!

(Coaching my daughter, Madelyn in soccer)

(Braeden's 4-year old baseball team when I was head coach. I am at in the back on the left, and Braeden is second one in from the left in the front)

SECOND TIME...MUCH BETTER

Let me expand on my story a bit, as it is one of second chances.

Let's fast-forward to the beginning of my sophomore year of college when a friend of mine (he was a walk-on the year before and made the baseball team) leans over to me in class and tells me that I need to try-out again. Hmmmmm...he must be joking, I thought! I proceeded to tell him that I had not touched a baseball in one year and didn't really see the point. He told me they were light on infielders and thought I should give it a shot anyway.

I went back to my dorm room and contemplated it. I talked to my family and friends about it. And what did I decide? Round 2...bring it on!!! What the heck? Why not? What are they going to do? Cut me? I know how to handle it this time!

Yet again I was called into the coach's office in the Creighton athletic department to find out if I made the team. It was then that, and I am starting to tear up again, that they asked me one of the most amazing things ...they asked me to be a full-time member of the Creighton baseball team!!!!!!! I have goose bumps as I write about this. I will never forget this!

I ended up playing my sophomore through senior year on the Creighton baseball team. It was one of the most amazing times in my life, and I thank God for that second chance.

(#15 during my senior year at Creighton)

I knew my college baseball days were coming to an end as we played those final few games my senior year. I knew I was not going on to play professional baseball.

But you know what, when that final out was recorded my senior year and it was officially over, that was okay with me. I was ready for it. Do you know why? I had been through this before. Four years earlier, baseball was taken from me and I had learned how to respond. I knew how to deal with my emotions. I knew what drove me in life and what I was going to do next. I knew how to fill the void. I was ready!

I have taken the lessons from both being cut from baseball, then later making the team, and I have used my reactions to formulate a plan for how I will handle change in the future. And now, when I am faced with change, I just activate my plan.

You need to make sure though that you are ready with your plan when you experience change or that transition comes. It will happen one day, so you might as well be prepared for it. Begin building your plan today for dealing with your emotions and filling the void!

ACTION ITEMS

Let's put these lessons into action! Please take some time to reflect on the following:

- How do you best actively and positively deal with your emotions? What are your top three emotional outlets?

- What interests do you have in life outside of sports/school/work? Write these down and then plan on how to make time for them.

A WORD FROM RUBEN GONZALEZ

"Always Have another Dream You are Pursuing"

Many athletes go into a deep depression after competing in the Olympics. They have been focused on the Olympic dream for years, and all of a sudden it's all over.

It happened to me after the Calgary Olympics and after the Albertville Olympics. You feel, "What now? How am I going to top this? Is my life going to be all downhill from now on?" You really get down after competing in the Olympics.

Believe it or not, over the years some Olympic medalists have committed suicide after the Olympics. Why? Because they did not have a plan for their life after sports.

I felt depressed and lost for several months after both the Calgary and the Albertville Olympics. My identity was so tied into being an athlete that I did not even know who I was. For six years after the Albertville Olympics, I drifted. I could not keep a job and I was a mess. Then, my Olympic luge coach talked me into coming out of retirement and trying to qualify for the 2002 Salt Lake City Olympics. Once again my life had a purpose. Once again I had a mission and a dream that inspired me to fight again.

After the Salt Lake Olympics, and after speaking at a neighborhood school and receiving amazing feedback, I had a brand new dream: to build a speaking business. Building my speaking business filled the void created by not competing athletically. Building my business fueled my competitive drive and kept me busy for twelve to eighteen hours each day for six years.

(Speaking for audiences around the world)

Because I had a new dream and purpose, I never got down or depressed after the Salt Lake City Olympics. I was too busy and driven to get depressed.

The fact that I spoke at that school was a blessing. It changed my life and gave it direction. It opened a whole new world for me. Since 2002 I have spoken for all kinds of corporations and organizations about how to become unstoppable in attaining your goals. I've spoken all around the world - South Africa, Tanzania, North Vietnam, Singapore, Japan, Mexico, Canada, Panama, Switzerland, Dubai, and many other places. My best selling books have been translated to Spanish, Romanian, German, Chinese, Indonesian, Polish, and more. And it all started with a little kid asking me to speak at his school.

God really does work in mysterious ways. I believe that he let me, a marginal athlete, get to compete in four Winter Olympics just so that I could spend the rest of my life teaching others how to realize their dreams.

After six years my business was strong and I looked for another challenge. After a second six year break, I re-entered the luge circuit and competed in the 2010 Vancouver Winter Olympics. But by then I had learned my lesson. I knew that I needed to have plans and dreams after the Olympics, and was prepared.

After the Vancouver Olympics we moved to Colorado and once again I have a new world I get to play in. I'm spending time with my kids hiking, climbing 14ers (mountains over 14,000 feet tall), and I'm learning how to snowboard, sail, play the guitar, and speak Italian. Learning new things and doing new things keeps me involved in life, gives my life meaning, and makes me happy.

Make a list of 100 things you'd like to do in your lifetime, a list of 100 places you'd like to visit, and 100 people you'd like to meet. Write them all down. Every time you do one of the things on your list put a big red checkmark next to it and write "Victory!" Over the years your lists will be full of victories and you will feel purposeful and happy.

Action Item Notes

Action Item Notes

5
BUILD YOUR "DREAM TEAM"

During my senior year of high school, it was apparent that our baseball team was going through a tough time. We were not winning the games we should have, and although we had all the right players and skills, our underperformance was just baffling. I felt that I needed to do something to re-unite this team.

During practice one day, I gathered the team together and pulled Sharpie pens, tongue depressors (like popsicle sticks), and athletic tape out of my baseball bag. Everyone was quiet, wondering what I had to say. "If we're going to make anything of this season, we have to come together. We need to play together and for each other. We must bond as a team. As you can see, I can break one tongue depressor easily," I said snapping the tongue depressor in half, "but if we tape all of these tongue depressors together, it becomes impossible to break. If we are all single tongue depressors, we will break easily, but bonded together, no one will break us!" I passed out the tongue depressors to each teammate and told each player to write their name on it, and when everyone was done, we put all the sticks together and wrapped the athletic tape around them. That became a symbol of the strength of our team, of our commitment to each other for that baseball season.

(Photo of Matt Phillips' family tongue depressors)

From that point on, that symbol was always prominently displayed during games. We always referred to it in the huddle before and after games because it helped bring us together. We started playing better and winning games. We came together as a team, understood our roles on the team, and executed our duties. As unfortunate as it was to lose during the Colorado State Baseball Tournament, the game right before the championship, I look back fondly on that season because of the turnaround we had as a team.

It may seem funny that tongue depressors brought a team together, but sometimes people need that spark to see the benefits of "team." It could have been tongue depressors…it could have been something very different…it didn't matter. We created something as a team to symbolize our commitment to excellence and to each other. Together we are always stronger!

Whether on the sporting field, at home, at work, or many other places in life, teams are key to success in life. Pulling together the right teams are crucial in our personal, professional, and spiritual lives as they provide us support, motivation, skill sets we don't necessarily have, and different perspectives than our own. They make us well-rounded and stronger than we can ever be alone.

WHAT "TEAMS" ARE IN YOUR LIFE?

Before delving into how to build a strong, effective, productive team, you need to understand that "teams" go beyond your playing field, court, ice, pitch, mat, or on whatever surface you play your sport. You must ensure the appropriate teams are in place to thrive in every aspect of your life.

Take a moment to think about all the teams you have in your life? Are you left just thinking about the sports you play? What about at work? At home? In your spiritual life?

Let me give you a few examples of which teams are in place (or should be in place) in your life to make you most successful.

Sports Teams

It doesn't matter if you are a gymnast or a baseball player, a sprinter or a football player, if you play an individual sport versus a team sport. You always have teams around you. It comes in the form of your coaches, teammates, trainers, and athletic staff.

Work Teams

You may have a team you work on or you may be part of a project team. Everyone plays a role on a team at work, whether you are a project manager, a subject-matter expert, a consultant, etc.

Family Teams

You are part of a family, your circle. My team began with my Dad, Mom, and sister. Now, I am married with three children and they are my team. We live, grow, laugh, and cry together. I rely on each person in my family to help me through the good and bad times in life. They are my ultimate team! They make me better every day!

Friend Teams

Do you have true friends in your life? I am not talking about acquaintances. I am talking about friends who, when the worst of the worst happens in your life, stand by you. I am talking about friends who challenge you to become better both on and off the field. I am talking about friends who celebrate the good and are there with you during struggles.

HOW DO YOU CREATE THE ULTIMATE TEAM?

UNDERSTANDING B³

Now that we understand all the teams that are in our lives, let's discuss how to properly build a team. Let's look into "**B³**" (B-cubed), my approach for setting up a successful team.

What does **B**³ stand for?

Build

Bond

Battle

All three go hand in hand. You can't have one without the other and they continuously change. If you are to be successful as a team, you must understand and employ each principle...**B**UILD...**B**OND...**B**ATTLE!

BUILD

Building a team is the initial stage of bringing that team together. When you build, you must have the following:

1. Clear, Identifiable Goal

Why are you bringing this team together? What is the team's purpose?

Pretend that I am a coach recruiting you. Which coach would you rather play for? Pick one of the following coach statements:

Statement #1: Our goal is to win some games this year.

Statement #2: We will win our division!

I don't know about you, but I pick the second statement. Win our division? I'm in. Now I can focus on how we get it done.

At Creighton University, my coach was phenomenal for setting out a clear goal for our team. We usually had two goals...1) to win our Conference and 2) to get to Regionals. Those were very clear goals for the team. After all, who doesn't understand what winning the Conference and getting to Regionals means?

You can see by these simple examples that when setting up a team, you need to first establish a clear, identifiable goal. You need each player or team member to understand what you are trying to achieve. Otherwise, people will a) just go through the motions or b) focus on their own personal goals, and the team will fail.

2. Rockin' Strategy

Once your team has a clear, identifiable goal, each team member needs to understand and to buy-in to the steps to reach that goal. You must have a fundamentally sound strategy!

It is not sufficient to simply state that you will win your division this year. What do you need in order to do this? How many games will you need to win? What does the schedule look like? What teams are you playing? What are their styles of play?

After setting our base goals at Creighton, our immediate next step was to talk about strategy, and we continued to talk about strategy for the rest of the season. We reviewed the teams we would play each week. We reviewed their playing style and who their key pitchers and hitters were. We understood the other team's game plan. We came up with a strategy for each game, and everyone on the team understood what we were trying to achieve long before we stepped on that field.

One thing is key regarding your strategy, whether in sports, business, or other aspects of life. You need 100% buy-in from each team member, otherwise you are wasting your time and everyone else's.

You are either in or you are out! Make a decision!

3. The Right Players

The other key aspect of building a team is to make sure that when you look around the room, you see all the right people there with you. You should be able to answer "Yes" to the following two questions: 1) "Would I go into battle with them?" and 2) "Do we have the right people for battle?"

Let's say your team was trying to compete in the all-around competition in gymnastics, but no one on your team knew how to vault. Sounds to me like you don't have the right players on your team.

You need to do whatever it takes to ensure that the key team players are with you in battle. This could mean recruiting someone for your team, teaching a teammate to play a new position or to develop a new skill. Without these team players, you may not be able to execute on your strategy and achieve your goal.

With a clear goal, a rockin' strategy, and the right players around you, your team will be ready for whatever challenge you are facing!

BOND

The team is now theoretically pulled together in that "Build" phase. Now it is time to **B**ond!

I am not going to tell you to hug it out now or even that you have to like everyone on your team. What I am going to tell you is that you need to understand how your team works, how people act and react to situations, and how to respectfully deal with each other.

Here are a few items to consider when bonding your team:

1. Get to know your teammates

The best way do this is through practice. The more times you practice together, the more you get to know your teammates style of play, their personality, and how they handle stress. You find out if they understand the team goals and are "all-in" for helping to achieve them.

It is also important to get to know your teammates off the field. Take some time to talk to these individuals and understand their lives. What kinds of things do they enjoy to do? What don't they like? What drives them day in and day out?

2. Understand your role

What is your role on the team? What is your job? What are your responsibilities on the team?

It is unbelievably important to understand the role you play on a team, and I am not just talking about what position you play or where you bat in the line-up. You need to understand how your personality and overall being fits into the team.

Let me give you an example. I played third base at Creighton University. The word "play" in my case may have a different meaning than yours. I rarely got to play or start in games at Creighton. I did much, much more practicing than actual playing in games.

So what was my role? My role was to get those starters ready to play every week. I was there to push those guys who started in front of me. I approached every day like I was the starter. I hustled everywhere on the field and constantly tried to outwork the other players. I would run bases in drills so the team could practice bunt coverages. I was willing to sacrifice my ego to help the team achieve our goals!

I am not telling you that you should try to remain in a back-up role if you are currently in one. I think you should try to work harder than everyone else to earn that starting spot! But, until that day comes when the coach gives you the "starting nod", understand your role and how it fits into what your team is trying to achieve.

I have to tell you that when I did get into those games to play, I took advantage of my opportunities! While getting the starters ready to play, I was preparing myself to play. And when the time came for me to execute upon my piece of the strategy, I was ready!

You can also be that spark your team needs at those key times, whether you are a starter or not. Perhaps you need to be the player that presents the team with tongue depressors, Sharpie pens, and athletic tape to bring your team together!

Here is a small illustration of the importance of bonding with your team. I think it is an amazing representation of how we should think of our teams... both on and off the sports field. You can use these with your sports team, of course, but also with your marriage, relationships, friends, and at work.

Side-by-Side
Standing side-by-side symbolizes your team walking into battle together. The line does not waiver in the face of war... it holds together and presses forward! Together you are ready for anything!

Back-to-Back
This illustration is simple...you have each other's back! You watch out for each other!

Face-to-Face
Standing face-to-face represents looking each other in the eye and challenging each other to become better! Not just to become better on the sporting field, but to be a better person, friend, son, daughter, uncle, aunt, employee, etc.

You need to look at your team and know that you would walk into battle together! You need to understand how each person will react when the battle begins, and know how to help each other through. Whether you are walking side-by-side, standing back-to-back, or standing face-to-face, you will be ready for war!

The Battle is coming! Get your team ready!

BATTLE

Now it's time to "Let 'Em Loose"!!!!!! Unleash the Beast!!!!! Let the battle commence.

You have built the team, bonded the team, and now you enter battle together. You must execute on your strategy...you must achieve your goal!

The Battle piece is probably the most fun for everyone, especially in sports. That's when you get to see if your preparation pays off, and if you have the right team and strategy in place. It's where the rubber meets the road!

1. Execute

Your team understands its goal and the strategy to reach its goal. Now it is time to execute! Utilize your team's cohesiveness to step up, and do what you know how to do and what you practiced.

2. Make changes along the way

One thing I have learned by playing sports, in business, and in life is that you need to constantly make adjustments when needed. I can't tell you how many times we expected to see one pitcher stroll out to the mound only to see someone else take the hill. Or, if you face a fastball thrower vs. a curveball pitcher, you may need to adjust your batting approach.

You cannot give up when you see something you don't expect. Make those small shifts in your approach to keep you on the road to achieving your goal!

3. Celebrate!!

Whether you win or lose a game, you MUST celebrate the successes along the way, no matter how small they seem. Celebrating these moments generates momentum! They get a taste of achieving that goal and they push harder to get there.

FOCUS ON THE POSITIVE!

CELEBRATE!

WHO'S IN CHARGE?

I hope you are sitting there right now asking yourself: "Who is in charge of each of the steps of **B**uild, **B**ond, and **B**attle?" The answer…EVERYONE! You, me, the person sitting next to you, the person you walk into battle with every day, the person who you challenge to improve, the person who challenges you to improve! EVERYONE!

If you think it is the coach's or parent's or friend's job to handle all of these items, you are sorely mistaken. It is everyone's responsibility on that team to drive each of those steps. Remember, you have all signed those tongue depressors! You wrapped those tongue depressors with athletic tape and bonded your team together! You are all-in! You have ownership in this team! You go = we all go!

If you have been sitting back waiting for something to spark your team, YOUR TIME IS NOW! Get up and do it! Drive them to excellence! Challenge each other! No more excuses! NONE!

Prepare your team today for success that no one can stop!

ACTION ITEMS

Let's put these lessons into action! We have discussed **B³** (Build, Bond, Battle) and it is time that you review the teams in your life to see if you are setting yourself and your teams up for success.

Please take some time to reflect on the following. For each team in your life, personally (at home), professionally (at work), and spiritually, answer the following items:

- Build

  - Do you have a clear, identifiable goal for your team?

  - Have you formulated the strategy (steps) to achieve your goal?

  - Do you have the right people on your team? What changes do you need to make?

- Bond

  - Have you taken time to get to know how your teammates act, react, and go about their day?

  - Do you understand your role on the team?

  - Will you walk into battle with your team?

• Battle

   - Are you holding up your end of the bargain and executing on your responsibilities?

   - Are you making adjustments to your strategy when necessary?

   - Are you celebrating the wins along the way?

A WORD FROM RUBEN GONZALEZ

"Create Your Own Dream Team"

One thing that sports teaches is that you can always achieve more if you are working as part of a team. Obviously, when I played soccer, I could not just think as an individual. I had to think about how my actions would affect my team. I was not a starter in my soccer team, and only played when we were up by two goals. So my role during the week was to help prepare the starters for game day and to inspire them to do their best through my work ethic and enthusiasm.

It also didn't take long after beginning to luge that I needed the help of a team. I was going to have to turn singles luge into a team sport by creating my own "Dream Team." The dream was to become an Olympian. The dream team would help me do it. My dream team was made up of coaches who helped me learn the sport, sled mechanics, chiropractors, doctors, and friends and family at home helping me financially and spiritually.

Creating a dream team helped me out in another way. After a bad crash, whenever I did not feel like taking another luge run, I did it anyways because I was not just doing it for myself. I was doing it for the team. We were going to go to the Olympics together.

When I was building my speaking business I did the same thing. I created a team of experienced speakers and authors and I met with them regularly to make sure I was on the right track. I still do this today. It's the mastermind principle. It's like having your own board of directors.

Iron sharpens iron. Create your own dream team. You'll be amazed at how much more you can accomplish.

Action Item Notes

Action Item Notes

6
YOUR ATTITUDE DEFINES YOU

"When you change the way you look at things, the things you look at change."
— Ralph Waldo Emerson

In elementary school, I had the great fortune to have my mother teach at our school, so it meant that my sister and I rode with our mom to grade school every day. I vividly remember my car rides, because on the way, my mom would make my sister and I say, "I like myself, I'm happy, and I'm going to have a good day". I didn't understand why she was making us say this silly phrase. It seemed lame to a 10 year old. But, I would say it every day before I got out of the car.

As we continued those rides to school, my mom discussed with us why she was having us say that phrase. She told us that we had a choice on how we approach our day and what type of attitude we carry with us. She told us that we can go through life with a positive attitude or a negative one, and that life is more fun, more productive, and more enjoyable with a positive attitude. My mom knew the importance of thinking positive and wanted to pass on that lesson to her children so we could also benefit from it.

Life can seem challenging and can be tough at times. Life can also seem easy and comfortable at times. We all experience ups and downs during our journey, and we all struggle with our attitude, as it slips from positive to negative and back again.

I have found over time, through sports and business, that my attitude determines how I approach challenges and adversity in my life, how I interact with those around me, and how I determine the future I want for myself. I have found time and time again that the more positive I am in my life, the more successful and happy I am.

Having a positive attitude comes down to two items:

1. Understanding a choice exists to either be positive or negative when you wake up in the morning

2. It is critical to surround yourself with the right people.

UNDERSTAND YOUR CHOICE

*"Nothing can stop the man with the right mental attitude
from achieving his goal; nothing on earth can help the man
with the wrong mental attitude." – Thomas Jefferson*

Every day you roll out of bed, you have a choice
about your attitude. You determine your attitude,
not someone else.

The reality is that as athletes, in life, and in business,
you face adversity and meet negative people who
challenge your attitude. Because of the tremendous
pressure in life, many people today, including athletes, tend to dwell on what went wrong in life instead of what went right. Their mind focuses on the
negative aspect of what happened. It could be not
performing as well as you wanted or your team los-
ing a key game. It might be not securing that key sale
or account. By dwelling on this past event, wrestling
with negative questions, or questioning your abilities, doubt begins. Negativity is a poison – it wrecks
the mind.

The reality is that negative things happen in life. We
face difficulty, loss, and disappointment. But, what
will define you in life is how you react to those tough
times. A positive attitude will energize you and the
people around you. It keeps you focused on contin-
ually improving, learning from the past, and making adjustments to improve in the future. It grounds

you, and then when adversity happens, which it will, it pushes you through that tough time. A positive attitude is like a powerful locomotive. Once that locomotive builds up momentum, it is hard to stop.

Focus on whatever you are going through right now, a success or struggle, and make that conscious decision to be positive! That's the first step. Next, take the time to reflect on what you did well in that situation. There is always something you did well…you just may not see it at first. Then look at what went wrong and ask yourself what you could have done differently. Finally, take what you have learned and make whatever changes are necessary and improve! The thoughts of the past are over because you are now focused on the present and making improvements to reach your goal.

Being positive is a process. In my baseball career, I had games, as does every baseball player, where I did not get a hit in a game (0 for 3 or 0 for 4). It is not fun. I remember getting down on myself after I had one of these games and dwelling on how poorly I hit the ball. I don't know when the trigger went off in my mind, and I think a lot of it was my parent's teaching finally creeping in, but I finally realized that I needed to focus on improving my swing so I had a better chance of getting a hit the next time. It was not beneficial to keep thinking about the tough at-bats.

Soon, I found that I would think about that last at bat for only a minute or so and then I was all about that next at bat and achieving my goal of getting a hit and helping my team win. The negativity that comes with looking back for too long was replaced by a positive focus, working in the present and looking towards the future.

Make a choice today to be positive! It is YOUR choice!

"Take charge of your attitude. Don't let someone else choose it for you." – Anonymous

SURROUND YOURSELF WITH POSITIVE PEOPLE

"Whatever you do in life, surround yourself with smart people who'll argue with you." – John Wooden

Taking that first step and making that choice to be positive in life is the biggest step. But, we cannot forget the importance of your surroundings, especially the people you associate with, as this has a huge impact on your attitude.

I strive to seek out individuals who exhibit critical personal characteristics that I also employ in my life. I search for individuals who have integrity, honesty, accountability to me and themselves, and humility. I try to find people who are responsible, respectful of me and themselves, compassionate, genuine, and supportive. And, we cannot forget positive attitude!

You need to find trusted individuals in your life who you can rely on to have your back and be a counsel to you when needed. These individuals should challenge you to improve, whether in sports, business, or life, and they comfort you in tough times as well.

Finding these types of people in life is tough, and you will find that most people only have a few true people like this in their lives. I can count mine on two hands. Between my Mom and Dad, sister, wife, best friend, and my uncles, those are the people I truly trust in my life to turn to in good times and bad.

These individuals, though, make me a better person, man, husband, father, brother, uncle, friend, worker, and follower of Jesus. It is worth the time to seek these individuals out in your life because you can believe in them and they will believe in you.

Belief...positive attitude...surrounding yourself with the right people...it is amazingly impactful!!

TIME TO CHOOSE

"If you don't like something, change it. If you can't change it, change your attitude." – Maya Angelou

This world is full of negativity at every turn. Be different. Be a game changer. Make a true impact. Be positive and display it proudly! Seek out positive people in your life! It's up to you!

"Your attitude, not your aptitude, will determine your altitude." – Zig Ziglar

ACTION ITEMS

Let's put these lessons into action! Take some time to reflect on the following. For each area in your life, personally, professionally, and spiritually, reflect on the following items:

- Where am I most positive in my life? In what ways am I positive? Why?

- What are areas where I struggle with negativity?

  - Why am I letting negativity get to me here? What is causing this?

- Am I surrounding myself with positive people in my life?

  - If not, who is a positive person and how do I connect with them?

- What words can I say to myself after I get out of bed in the morning to start my day off positively?

A WORD FROM RUBEN GONZALEZ

"Protect Your Attitude"

Your attitude is your frame of mind. It's whether you decide to focus on the positive side of what's happening to you or on the negative side. Reread

the last sentence - your attitude is a decision. It's your choice.

Yes, your attitude is your decision. And if you choose to have a negative attitude, your results will suffer. A positive attitude does not guarantee success, but you will always be more successful with a positive attitude than with a negative one.

Protect your attitude. Because it can take you to new heights or take you down and knock you out.

A year and a half before the 2002 Salt Lake City Olympics, I was in St. Moritz, Switzerland for a World Cup luge race. I was not having any major problems on that track but because of a loss of concentration during the race I had a terrible crash at over 80 MPH.

I totaled my sled and broke bones in my foot and my hand. For the next three days I got myself into a pity party. "Why me? I can't afford another sled and I'm hurt just a season before the Olympics. This is not fair! I'll never make it to the Olympics now."

(Bad day at the track - broken bones and totaled sled)

I got so down on myself that nobody wanted to be around me. Have you noticed that when you have a pity party no one wants to come?

Finally, three days later, halfway across the Atlantic on the way back home I got my head straight. I realized that, heck, I've broken bones before and bones heal so a broken bone is just a temporary inconvenience. And, I may not be able to afford a new sled but maybe I can borrow a sled from another luger.

The next day, when I got home I went back to the gym. I could not lift as much with my casts but mentally I was back in the game. Then I started calling all my luge buddies to see if they had a sled they could lend me.

Adam Cook, a member of the New Zealand Luge Team lent me his sled. Adam is quite a bit shorter than I am and his sled was really small, but I decided that I would focus on the positive—at least I now had a sled.

I went on to qualify and compete in the Salt Lake City Olympics on Adam's little sled.

Decide that you will have a positive attitude so that you can achieve your goals faster, more easily, and so you can be the best that you can be.

Action Item Notes

Action Item Notes

7
HOW TO RAISE YOUR SELF-BELIEF LEVEL

"There are three things extremely hard: steel, a diamond, and to know one's self."
— Ben Franklin

I want you to do a little exercise. Get up and find a mirror. Stand directly in front of it, and answer these questions:

• What do you see when you are standing in front of a mirror?

• What do you think of the person standing in front of you?

• Are you proud of what you see?

• Are you disappointed by what you see?

• Do you really know who that person is in front of you?

• Do you truly understand what makes yourself tick?

• What energizes you?

• What makes you get out of bed in the morning?

• What are you going to be in life?

• What are you going to do with your life?

• How do you want others to describe you?

• How would you describe yourself?

• Who are you?

Tough questions, aren't they? Yet these are vital questions that not only every athlete, but every individual needs to be asking themselves.

As human beings, we can be extremely hard on ourselves. It comes in the form of what we think we look like on the outside and how we act and react on the inside. We pick apart every part of ourselves, inside and out, and compare ourselves to everyone else around us. And it is at these times when we decide whether we are passing or failing in each area.

You hear it all the time in life and in sports:

"I wish I was a little thinner."

"I wish I was a fast as that person."

"I don't like how my body looks."

"I am not as good looking as him/her."

"My muscles should be big like that other person."

"I am not as smart as that other person."

"I am not good enough."

"I'll never be as good at _____(fill in the blank)."

"I wish I was better."

These comments can be detrimental to self-image and lead to unnecessary damage ourselves.

When I played college baseball, I analyzed every part of each game and my opponents. I remember comparing myself to other teammates, some of whom were much stronger and faster than me. How was I going to compete with these fast guys? How does that guy swing the bat so fast? How is he so much stronger than me?

As I asked myself these questions, emotions ranging from positive to negative flooded in. Sometimes I would tell myself that I can get that hit because I was mentally and physically ready. I would focus on the gifts God gave me and try to use them to the best of my ability. I would stay focused on positive thoughts about myself.

Other times, I started to doubt the way God made me because maybe I wasn't as tall as the other guys, or I wasn't as strong as them. I would start doubting my ability to even hit a baseball because my swing was not fast enough or I was afraid of looking dumb if I did not get a hit. I would think of what that other person thought of me (even if they weren't thinking that) and I would lose focus on who I was as a player and a person. My negative thoughts sabotaged my performance on the field.

No matter what we are facing in life, we must find a way to believe in ourselves. We must surround ourselves with people who believe in us. We must be kind to ourselves!

POSITIVE BELIEF IN YOURSELF

"If you hear a voice within you say "you cannot paint," then by all means paint, and that voice will be silenced." – Vincent Van Gogh

When all is said and done, we have a choice on how we are going to think and act. We have a choice on whether we will react positively or negatively to how we look and feel. You have a choice whether you will say, "I am proud of what I am looking at" or "I don't like what I see" when you are staring into that mirror.

Even though it was hard for me while playing sports and still even today, I try to take a positive approach regarding my self-image. A lot of this, of course, has been learned over the years and was instilled in me by my parents, but I choose to be positive.

When I was playing college baseball, and was worried about others around me, I had to force myself to change my thinking and switch from negative to positive thoughts. I started focusing on myself and what I needed to do to improve my skills in a positive way so that I would be ready for each opportunity to play. I would ask myself, "Did I work as hard as I could today?" "Did I get everything I could out of that practice or weight lifting session?" This grounded me in my work ethic and I walked off the field with a smile on my face knowing that I took advantage of every opportunity on that practice field to prepare me for the games and to set me up for success.

Was it easy? No! Do I still struggle with it today? Yes! Negative thoughts still find their way into my mind, no matter what the area of my life. It could be while I coach my kids in sports, in my career, or with my faith. But no matter the situation, I still ask the same questions of myself: "Did I work as hard as I could today?" "Did I get everything I could out of that experience?" "How did I show myself appreciation today?" "Did I make me proud today?" This continues to ground me, and then I know I did everything I could, in a healthy way.

We all need to take more time to focus on ourselves, our talents, and the gifts God has given us. We need to be proud of ourselves inside and out, and know that we are special in God's eyes.

HELP, PLEASE!

"Don't walk behind me; I may not lead. Don't walk in front of me; I may not follow. Just walk beside me and be my friend."
— *Albert Camus*

One of the most powerful ways to raise our self-belief level is to surround ourselves with people who believe in us!

I have discovered over time that when I begin to doubt myself, it is extremely useful to speak with someone. Although it may be awkward to approach these individuals at times, I know I would have reacted differently had I not talked about my problems with trusted people. It helped me to not only verbalize what I was going through (saying it out loud really does help), but the positive feedback and outside perspective I would get from these people would bring me back to reality.

I would not be the same person I am today without the family and friends in my life. From my parents and sister, to my wife and uncles, to a few "true" friends, all these people took the time to care about me and listen to me when I was struggling. I think it is so important that you have a network of people who believe in you and can support and encourage you in life's adventures! It comes down to finding good people who are with you in the good times and bad, and give you a different perspective. These people ground you when you seem out of control.

BE KIND TO YOURSELF

All of this boils down to the Golden Rule…"Treat others how you want to be treated." We want others to love us and to care about us. We want others to respect us and treat us kindly.

When thinking about self-image, I will twist the Golden Rule wording a bit to "Treat yourself how you want others to treat you." We need to be kind to ourselves. We need to treat ourselves with respect. We need to love and care about ourselves.

We are so hard on ourselves, constantly analyzing how we look, how we feel, and how we compare to others around us. But you need to be sure that you are treating yourself with respect, dignity, care, and love. That is the only way that you are going to push through the tough times and go even further in the good times. Treat yourself kindly! Be positive! Life is great! Life brings challenges, but out of every trial comes a lesson to be learned and true growth in character. Embrace those challenges and enjoy the ride!

ACTION ITEMS

Let's put these lessons into action! Reflect on the following questions:

- Do you believe in yourself? Why or why not?

    - For those areas where you struggle, how can you improve on self-belief?

- What people in your life believe in you?

- Are you being kind to yourself? Why or why not?

    - How can you be even more kind to yourself?

    - What exercises can you do every day to remind yourself that you are special?

A WORD FROM RUBEN GONZALEZ

"How You See Yourself will Determine the Heights You will Reach"

When I was six years old my family moved from Argentina to Queens, New York. School was tough for me because I was the only kid in my class who did not speak English. Other kids picked on me because I was the kid who did not talk to anybody.

After a while I started to think that there was something wrong with me. My self-image was awful.

Thinking I was inferior was a mistake on my part. You should never let another person's opinion of you to become your reality. But I was just a little kid and didn't know any better. I just thought there was something wrong with me.

My poor self image turned me into an over achiever because I was trying to prove to myself that I was OK. I was a tall guy with a Napoleonic Complex. I became an Olympian to make myself feel worthy. Believe it or not, I did not start feeling comfortable with who I was until I was a three-time Olympian. That shows how small those kids in grade school made me feel.

Thank God I finally recovered. Having a poor self image is a terrible thing to live with. Today, I feel so empowered, so powerful, so free to just be myself.

Here are a few tips to help you improve your self-image.

1 - Don't ever compare yourself to others. When you do, you are fooling yourself because invariably you will compare your weaknesses to other people's strengths. That's not fair to you and doing so will only hurt your self-image.

2 - Stand up for yourself. Don't be afraid to show your anger when you feel angry or disrespected. Make people respect you. When someone disrespects you, call them on it. Don't let them get away with it.

3 - Protect your time. It's your most valuable asset. Be willing to say no to anything that will keep you from realizing your dreams and goals. You don't have to apologize for having your own dreams and plans.

4 - Associate with high achievers and winners. Successful people will help you reach your goals and dreams and they will always be encouraging.

Finally, remember that God made you the way you are for a reason. God put a dream in your heart, and he equipped you with all the skills, talents, and gifts you will need to reach that dream. God has a plan for your life, and he did not create any junk. You were made in God's image and you have the seeds of greatness within you.

Action Item Notes

Action Item Notes

ACKNOWLEDGEMENTS

I first must thank Ruben Gonzalez for asking me to write this book with him. Writing this book has been one of the most incredible experiences of my life, but without Ruben's idea, I never would have done this. Thanks, Ruben!

Also a big thank you to my wife, Shannon, for allowing me to take time to write this book, as this was a sacrifice for both of us. Shannon is the most incredible mother and wife, and I thank God every day for her.

Most of all, I give thanks to God for putting amazing people in my life, including my wife, children, Mom, Dad, sister, and the rest of my wonderful family and friends. God has also put numerous, incredible athletes in my path, including Ruben. I cherish the time I have gotten to spend with each of them and I am now lucky to call many of them friends.

Thank you, God, for all you have done in my life.

Love,
Matt

"If God is for us, who can ever be against us?" – Romans 8:31

AUTHOR BIOS

MATT PHILLIPS

As a former Bundesliga (first league) professional base-ball player for the Diving Ducks in Wiener Neustadt, Austria and college base-ball player at Creighton University in the United States, Matt has been on an amaz-ing journey through sports and life. Beyond his sports career, Matt has worked with  numerous Fortune 500 companies in operations, accounting, and finance, and these roles have taken him all over the United States and Europe.

As a keynote speaker, workshop leader, and coach, Matt uses his sports and business experience to in-spire individuals to prioritize their lives or business-es, to get back to what is most important to them, and to push beyond whatever limitation that lies in their paths. It is all about living life to the full-est! Matt inspires audiences and individuals with his passion for sharing his story and personal life lessons as experienced through sports and business (www.matt-phillips.net).

Matt is also the President and Co-Founder of Lasting Crown (www.lastingcrown.com), a non-profit organization focused on addressing the issues athletes face by connecting them to God and each other.

RUBEN GONZALEZ

 A seemingly "ordinary guy," Ruben Gonzalez wasn't a gift-ed athlete. Inspired by watch-ing Scott Hamilton, Ruben took up the sport of luge when he was 21. Against all odds, four years and a few broken bones later, he was competing in the Calgary Winter Olym-pics. At the age of 47 he was racing against 20-year-olds in the Vancouver Olym-pics, becoming the first person to ever compete in four Winter Olympics each in a   different decade - 1988, 1992, 2002, 2010.

His best-selling book, *The Courage to Succeed*, has been translated to Spanish, German, Polish, Chinese, Indonesian and several other languages.

Ruben is the founder of OlympicMotivation.com a firm dedicated to inspiring and equipping people to achieve their goals.

A master storyteller and keynote speaker, Ruben uses his Olympic experiences to inspire audiences to think differently, live life with passion and have the courage to take the necessary steps toward their goals – to push beyond self-imposed limitations and to produce better results.

"If you will listen to Ruben speak or read his book, your life will change." - Lou Holtz - Legendary Notre Dame Coach

17817323R00062

Made in the USA
Charleston, SC
02 March 2013